The Manager's Pocket Guide to
Effective
Mentoring

Dr. Norman H. Cohen

HRD Press
Amherst, Massachusetts

Published by:

HRD Press
22 Amherst Road
Amherst, MA 01002
1-800-822-2801 (U.S. and Canada)
413-253-3488
413-253-3490 (FAX)
www.hrdpress.com

ISBN 0-87425-469-8

Cover design by Eileen Klockars
Editorial services by Robie Grant
Production services by Clark Riley

PRINTED IN CANADA

TABLE OF CONTENTS

This Pocket Guide is designed for use by the mentor practitioner. The information has been specifically arranged in a format that should provide quick access to the basic concepts and techniques applicable to the mentoring model of learning.

✳

General Introduction: *The Manager's Pocket Guide to Effective Mentoring*

General Introduction:
The Manager's Pocket Guide to Effective Mentoring

Purpose

The Manager's Pocket Guide to Effective Mentoring has been specifically designed to promote the art of effective mentoring practice. Mentors can refer to it as a source of pragmatic advice during their interpersonal involvement with mentees.

In addition to offering immediate guidance that mentors can use to maximize their contribution to the development of significant mentee competencies, *The Pocket Guide* also provides a comprehensive explanation of the mentoring model as a valuable source of learning within the modern workplace.

As a carefully organized sourcebook, *The Pocket Guide* is presented in a format that allows mentors rapid access to important concepts and techniques they can directly utilize in assisting mentees to:

(1) participate in constructive dialogues during the entire mentoring experience

(2) map out attainable personal and professional goals

(3) analyze problems, formulate realistic solutions, and make constructive decisions

(4) plan workable strategies for pursuing career, training, and educational development

(5) implement positive actions to achieve stated objectives

Mentoring Today

The Pocket Guide presents an expanded view of the traditional concept of mentoring by examining the behavioral expertise now required by modern mentors.

Today, mentors are clearly faced with the difficult challenge of establishing and sustaining meaningful mentoring relationships in an often intensely competitive world. Due to the increased speed, scope, and depth of change, people are confronted daily with a multiplicity of new demands on their mental ability and judgment, psychological stability, and emotional resiliency.

For a large number of individuals, the compressed transition time between even the recent past and the immediate present has created a condition of considerable situational stress. By sponsoring a variety of mentoring initiatives, many leaders of our culture have certainly recognized their responsibility by actively supporting programs devoted to the growth of adaptable, productive, and mature citizens.

However, to participate as intelligent and skilled practitioners, it is critical that mentors redefine and adapt the powerful opportunity available through the classic one-to-one model of interaction to the unique needs of our contemporary adult learners, who must function within more complex workplace, academic, social, and personal environments.

Organization of Work
The *Manager's Pocket Guide to Effective Mentoring* is organized to:

(1) provide a precise orientation to highly significant points mentors must initially understand about the one-to-one approach to learning

(2) present a concise overview of the complete mentor role

(3) clarify the idea of phases in the mentoring relationship

(4) explain in detail the particular relevance and application of the six mentor dimensions

(5) offer guidance in maintaining a mentee journal

(6) suggest learning activities for mentees

(7) allow mentors to reference the *Principles of Adult Mentoring Inventory* as a carefully selected source of effective mentor behaviors

(8) provide an outline of the six mentoring dimensions for quick review

Additional Information about Mentoring
The titles of materials particularly dedicated to promoting the mentoring model of learning are

included in the "About the Author" biography at the end of this book. Although *The Pocket Guide* can be used as a self-contained work, mentor practitioners as well as scholars and researchers could certainly benefit from the information and approach described in the other publications.

The Mentor Role: An Introduction

The Mentor Role:
An Introduction

The Six Mentoring Dimensions

The mentor role refers to the deliberate use of six types of behavior during an evolving interpersonal relationship with a mentee. The diagram below highlights the synergistic potential of these six dimensions.

It is important to recognize that the mentor role is a dynamic, pragmatic approach to, and not just a theoretical view of, a mentor's involvement with a mentee.

The mentoring model of learning is usually initiated to increase the mentee's development of competencies and options, and relies on the integration of two major components: (1) constructing meaningful dialogues and (2) designing tangible actions.

Relationship Dimension	Informative Dimension
Complete	
Facilitative Dimension **Mentor** Confrontive Dimension	
Role	
Mentor Model Dimension	Employee Vision Dimension

There are four important points about mentoring which should be used as basic guidelines when applying this model:

(1) *Planned Sessions*—Mentoring sessions must be planned to ensure that an adequate *number* of mentor-mentee meetings is scheduled, and that a sufficient amount of *time* is allocated for meaningful dialogue and activities.

(2) *Holistic Experience*—From the mentee's point of view, mentoring can be properly understood as a holistic experience which results from the interaction between the mentor and mentee over an extended timeframe. The primary influence the mentor exerts on the mentee is that of advocate for constructive change and positive growth.

In this critical role, the mentor assumes responsibility that is similar to the traditional profile of the fully engaged adult educator. Successful mentors attempt to utilize all six mentoring dimensions competently during their relationships with mentees.

(3) *Active Participation*—Instead of relying on the assumed power of the mentor as an elevated role model influencing unknown protégés from a distance, the mentoring model of active learning requires participation in direct dialogues and shared activities as a means of promoting the mentee's personal and professional development. Often, mentors make an important difference because they act as face-to-face stabilizing influences who help mentees transition through significant life and workplace events.

4

(4) *Ideal vs. Realistic*—The ideal situation for a mentor would be the opportunity and ability to function well in all six of the mentor dimensions over time. However, while striving to achieve the conscious balance implied by the complete mentor role, even the truly committed and skilled mentor should remember that mentoring is a performance art which usually occurs under less than ideal conditions. So "complete" should not be equated with "perfect."

In addition, even a talented and properly trained mentor may not be able to achieve the objectives of the complete mentor role, simply because the mentor cannot control all of the relevant variables that might affect the typical mentoring situation.

Important elements the mentee brings to the mentoring experience, such as initial interpersonal maturity, self-confidence, reaction to stress, ability to benefit from constructive feedback, and personal determination to succeed are all components that can directly impact the possibility of a successful mentoring relationship.

A mentor should be prepared to contribute as much as possible to the development of the mentee, but without imposing or forcing the idea that all mentees must experience the complete mentor role for the mentoring relationship itself to be considered as a worthwhile learning opportunity.

As unique individuals, mentees will certainly vary in their ability to take advantage of the benefits offered by the mentoring model of learning.

✳ The Complete Mentor Role: Actions and Purpose

The Complete Mentor Role:
Actions and Purpose

Introduction

The following explanation briefly describes each of the six separate dimensions of mentoring that, when integrated over time, constitute the profile of an individual functioning in the *complete* mentor role.

This section focuses on the specific behavioral actions and primary purpose relevant to each dimension. The material is organized to provide quick access to the essentials of effective mentoring practice.

New practitioners might want to review the material immediately before a mentoring session.

1. Relationship Dimension

Behavior   *Purpose*

*Empathetic Listening ------- *communicate sincere interest*

*Open-ended Questions ------ *express immediate concerns*

*Descriptive Feedback --------------- *give observations only*

*Perception Checks--------------------- *comprehend feelings*

*Nonjudgmental Responses ---- *control emotions/reactions*

2. Informative Dimension

Behavior   *Purpose*

*Questions about Present ---- *learn facts about job/career*

*Review of Background ------- *develop work-related profile*

*Probing Questions--------------- *require concrete answers*

*Directive Comments ---------- *present problems/solutions*

*Restatements ----------------------- *ensure accuracy/clarity*

*Reliance on Fact ---------------------- *integral for decisions*

3. Facilitative Dimension

Behavior   *Purpose*

*Hypothetical Questions ---------- *expand individual views*

*Uncovering of Assumptions ---------- *provide information/ experience*

*Multiple Viewpoints ------------ *analyze decisions/options*

*Examining Commitment ----------- *provide foundation for serious achievement of goals*

*Analysis of Reasons ------ *learn basis* for *current pursuits*

*Review of Preferences -------------- *specific to work/career*

4. Confrontive Dimension

Behavior   *Purpose*

*Careful Probing ----------- *assess psychological readiness*

*Open Acknowledgment - *express concerns about criticism*

*Verbal Discrepancies--- *self-assessment of goals/actions*

*Selective Behaviors -- *discuss likely strategies for change*

*Attention to Feedback-----------*limit constructive criticism*

*Comments about Potential------ *reinforce belief in growth*

5. Mentor Model Dimension

Behavior   *Purpose*

*Offering Thoughts/Feelings ----------- *learn from difficulty*

*Selecting Related Examples ----------- *provide experiences that motivate*

*Realistic Belief in Ability ------ *commit to attainable goals*

*Confident View of Risk---------------- *accept as necessary for opportunities*

*Statements about Action ------ *encourage direct initiatives*

6. Employee Vision Dimension

Behavior   *Purpose*

*Reflection on Present/Future------------ *reflect on career/ training/education*

*Questions about Change ----- *clarify perceptions/abilities*

*Review of Choices---------------- *assess options/resources*

*Comments about Strategies ---- *analyze decision making*

*Expressions of Confidence ------------- *believe in carefully thought out plans*

*Respect for Capacity ---------- *trust in ability to determine personal future*

*Encouragement about Dreams----------- *develop talents/ seek goals*

Phases of the Mentoring Relationship

Phases of the Mentoring Relationship

Introduction

Mentees should experience the personality of a mentor partner as dynamic rather than static.

An experienced and proficient mentor would ideally be capable of functioning with reasonable competence in the complete mentor role at the first session. Of course, not all mentors will be seasoned practitioners, and as continuing learners themselves, they will benefit from three directly related and enriching events:

(1) ongoing one-on-one interaction with mentees
(2) self-reflection and assessment regarding their own mentoring practice
(3) the opportunity provided by training programs to engage in critiques and receive feedback from their more knowledgeable mentor peers

However, it is important to recognize that in applying the term *phases* to mentoring, the focus must remain on the mentee as the primary adult learner and beneficiary of the mentor's experience.

Certainly, a simultaneous training program provided by the sponsoring organization to enhance mentoring skills will make a meaningful difference, because skilled mentors understand how to effectively approach mentees at every stage as capable participants in the mutual attempt to improve proficiencies mentees themselves have identified and agreed to develop.

Concept of Phases

The concept of phases should be primarily interpreted as the continual personal and professional development *of mentees* as they move through the extended timeframe of mentor-mentee dialogues and activities.

In applying the idea of phases to the mentoring context, the central assumption is that as their relationship matures, the potential for the mentor to engage the mentee in more complex mutual interaction will increase *because* the mentee has also personally responded constructively to the positive potential within the framework of the ongoing relationship.

New mentors should be aware that in attempting to function as practitioners of the complete mentor role, it is the *mentees' own readiness to participate* at every stage that also must remain the central reference point to guide proper mentoring behavior.

The outline that follows should be utilized as a simplified reference to track the probable momentum over time of a representative mentor-mentee learning experience. Moreover, the concept of phases should be considered as particularly applicable to the one-year model of planned mentoring interaction that is typical of many sponsored programs.

16

Outline of Phases

Early:

Relationship Dimension -------------------------- Trust

Middle:

Informative Dimension-------------------------- Advice

Later:

Facilitative Dimension -------------------- Alternatives

Confrontive Dimension --------------------- Challenge

Last:

Mentor Model Dimension------------------ Motivation

Employee Vision Dimension ----------------- Initiative

Applying the Six Mentor Dimensions

Applying the Six Mentor Dimensions

Introduction
The following material highlights the key concepts and essential behaviors associated with the six critical mentoring functions.

For each of the separate dimensions, a broad range of possibilities are offered to illustrate the different scenarios mentors could encounter within the anticipated boundaries of that particular category. Also, representative examples are provided to accurately portray the important mentor-mentee interactions most likely to occur with a specific phase.

This section is designed to offer mentors a source of information—from the unique perspective of this model of learning— that they can utilize as a reference point to guide them through the basic reasoning and strategies important to mentoring decisions.

1. Relationship Dimension

Key Concept: *Trust*

Essential Behaviors:
*Sharing/Reflecting
*Empathetic Listening
*Understanding/Acceptance

Introduction

There are numerous possibilities regarding the initial session. The variations could run the gamut from an actual first-time meeting to the reintroduction of persons who are already reasonably familiar, though not as a pair formally defined as mentor and mentee.

Also, the mix of individuals could vary from mentors and mentees who have a variety of experiences with mentoring to those with limited reference points and no fixed opinions.

For those with prior involvement, some may have had past mentoring relationships in which their goals were constructively realized, while others may report a history of less than uniformly growth-enhancing or even of very disappointing contact.

Moreover, the participants could range from the open-minded and receptive to those who appear resistant to the announced program objectives and still invested in substituting their own erroneous expectations.

Familiarity—Pluses and Minuses
With respect to the specific issue of familiarity, the extent of background commonality may have a significant positive or negative influence on the direction of the evolving relationship. For example, if the participants know each other reasonably well, this reference point could enable both mentor and mentee to move reasonably quickly into direct issues such as specific goal planning and identification of immediate work-related development activities.

Barriers
However, the same familiarity useful in accelerating the action planning and learning curve could also act as a subtle barrier between the pair, who may repeat some aspects of their prior relationship which detract from the mentor-mentee experience.

For example, if the pair had been previously associated as manager and subordinate, then they might approach current issues and concerns from the perspective of the older relational situation rather than engage in the collaborative interpersonal interaction more suitable to mentoring.

It may therefore be necessary for the mentor to openly redefine the present purpose of their new involvement by specifically explaining the differences between the goals of mentor/mentee involvement and their previous professional contacts.

Minimal or No Prior Contact

If no significant history exists between the pair, then the mentor can rely on the basic techniques of relationship emphasis. Early in the developing relationship, it is especially important that mentors concentrate on posing brief, open-ended questions and encouraging the mentee to answer in adequate detail.

The use of empathetic listening is particularly helpful because it usually creates a positive environment of acceptance and calmness, and thereby enables the mentor to obtain an accurate understanding of the mentee's unique point of view.

The Need to Create Trust

Whatever the interpersonal climate of the actual starting point, it is vital that the mentor initially approach the mentee from the general perspective of the mentoring model of learning.

Even if constructive reference points are part of their mutual background, the prudent mentor should be prepared to develop rather than to assume that the trust required to build the foundation essential for a meaningful mentoring relationship already exists.

24

Also, it is worth noting that trust may not be automatically or easily bestowed by every mentee. And such caution by a mentee may not signal a cynical attitude, but rather may reflect a skeptical reluctance based on real-world experience that questions whether good intentions always translate into productive outcomes.

Of course, both a foolish naivete and an ingrained mistrust can create problems for genuine mentoring, which is itself centered in honest and reflective dialogue.

The Mentee Experience—Acceptance vs. Invalidation

Another consideration for the mentor is the need to guard against a too rapid response to opinions and statements offered by the mentee, especially in the early part of the relationship.

In addition to listening carefully, as well as to phrasing questions that demonstrate sensitivity, mentors should also be alert to inadvertently creating the impression that they are reacting with instant disapproval to the views of mentees.

In fact, a mentor may not personally agree with a mentee's ideas or attitudes. And the mentee may truly benefit from a challenge to an unsupportable belief or narrow perspective based on limited exposure to a complex world. But, in such cases, it is important that mentors refrain from too quickly communicating their very different interpretations of reality, because some mentees may actually interpret what mentors intend to be Socratic dialogues as harsh disputes in which their point of view is rapidly dismissed or overridden.

Refrain from Instant Disagreement

A willingness to hear the mentee out and to refrain from instant disagreement will communicate the critical acceptance dimension so necessary to the creation of trust between the participants. By accepting the mentee's legitimate right to hold very personal and different views, the mentor conveys the relevant message that the mentee is respected as a unique individual.

Mentors must remember that mutual agreement regarding ideas and beliefs may not occur between themselves and mentees, and that such an agenda should not necessarily be viewed as the primary goal of mentoring.

The ability to constructively debate differences, however, should in fact be considered a paramount benefit of such spirited exchanges. The goals of mentoring are not conversion and cloning; they are learning and reflection.

Timing of Remarks

A significant decision made by the skilled mentor should be attention to the proper *timing* of direct challenges to the mentee's facts and opinions.

The mentor must be particularly alert to the timing of an intervention—especially when utilizing the confrontive approach—because the mentor is relying as much on the psychologically right moment to introduce a point as much as on the actual intellectual weight of the issue under consideration.

Similar to the idea of a teachable moment, it is sometimes nearly impossible to separate the value of the comment from the readiness of the receiver to hear it. Mentors should be careful in the important early stages of the relationship that good intentions do not unexpectedly but dramatically transform into missed opportunities and even negative outcomes.

For example, a mentor who exposes—before a reasonable degree of trust has been established—a mentee's thin veneer of facts or legitimate experiences could clearly be successful in winning an argument but deficient in the goal of assisting the mentee to reexamine flawed or poorly reasoned conclusions.

Mentors need to be properly concerned about implying that their own more sophisticated and seasoned reference points must always be automatically adopted as gospel.

Avoid Inappropriate Competition

Mentors should also be careful to avoid the unfortunate trap of arguing with mentees as if the rationale were to score debate points. Ideally, mentees should be openly encouraged to reevaluate their opinions and beliefs, especially if they are derived from a background that is truly limited in depth and scope. However, mentors also should be alert to the disservice of intellectually jousting mentees into a more compliant position; this type of engagement could inadvertently place mentees in the difficult situation of feeling almost compelled to dismiss or invalidate their own history as a source of legitimate reference.

Such a polarizing and competitive agenda could introduce a most unwelcome element into the early mutual contact because the mentor could end up as a patronizing or condescending authority figure and the mentee as a person whose self-confidence is undermined rather than strengthened.

2. Informative Dimension

Key Concept: *Advice*

Essential Behaviors:

* Learning facts about career/ education/plans/progress
* Commenting on use of information
* Providing tailored/accurate/ sufficient knowledge

Introduction

A central concern of the informative dimension is the reliance on *facts*. Until they have formulated a reasonably substantial factual profile of mentees, mentors should refrain from proposing immediate solutions. An instant answers approach to concerns, issues, and goals is usually inconsistent with the slower process of collecting adequate knowledge about another person.

Avoid the Quick Fix

Astute mentors should therefore offer serious advice with caution and even reluctance in the initial phase to ensure that the legendary "one size fits all" pattern does not intrude and thereby hinder or prevent genuinely meaningful guidance from being realized.

In particular, mentors should be prepared to resist the pressure exerted by mentees in stressful situations who desire quick-fix responses to all problems.

Be Alert to Old Patterns

A mentor may sometimes discover that a mentee's current inability to carefully collect information, to consider sensible options and probable consequences, and to pursue workable alternatives is directly connected to an overreactive history of dealing with basic as well as complex issues.

In such cases, mentees could greatly benefit from exposure to a more rational and reflective approach, especially when the stress response is generated more by internal anxiety than by a realistic appraisal of external conditions.

Mentees who appear to be suffering from this type of stress reaction and subsequent overload need to learn more productive coping strategies, especially with regard to the often difficult task—intellectual as well as emotional—of developing a more objective, comprehensive view of empirical events rather than relying exclusively on the often narrow conclusions of subjective perception and personal interpretation.

Mentees who habitually overreact are often unable to distinguish minor from major problems, and expend maximum personal energy daily on events that only require minimum exertions. Then they are often too fatigued and overwrought to deal with truly significant concerns.

Of course, when there also are real-world conditions that account for the high degree of situational stress, mentors should certainly consider referring mentees to qualified mental health professionals as well for specific assistance with life and work issues.

Mentors can be pragmatic role model resources as they demonstrate the factual art of striving for an analytical appraisal of problems as well as for balanced and functional solutions.

Tailored Advice, Not Platitudes

Mentors should recall the unfortunate ease with which they can offer general advice to those who are essentially unknown—but not unknowable—persons requesting their assistance, and refrain from speaking too quickly.

In worst case scenarios, even mentors with impeccable intentions can resort to an undemanding reliance on platitudes instead of the tailored advice that depends on a solidly grounded and detailed informational profile of the mentee.

To prevent the use of generalities, mentors can specifically utilize the data provided by mentees in the initial sessions regarding such basic matters as prior education, training, and work experience as a factual foundation.

In addition, the views of mentees regarding their career and academic aspirations should be solicited directly. Even in the preliminary stages of interpersonal interaction, it is important to ensure that the planning effort is based on a coherent, data-based model of reality.

Use of the Mentee Profile Form

The *Mentee Profile Form* can be utilized to reveal a portrait of a mentee's past background, present objectives and concerns, and future plans.

The mentee can be asked to complete the form before the first meeting (if possible) to accelerate the introductory stage of the mentoring process, as well as to provide a concrete reference point around which to center the dialogue of the early sessions.

Mentors will often find that locating the focus of the initial discussions in tangible issues can prevent the impression some mentees report of abstract, unproductive, and time-consuming meandering rather than focused meetings that identify pathways appropriate to their own individual and unique perspective.

By using the form, mentors can identify the mentee's various goals early in the relationship, and then later in the facilitative phase, for example, initiate a productive examination of the correlation between mentees' plans and their actual resources (financial, family, organizational) for achieving particular objectives.

The following model of the *Mentee Profile Form* can be used as part of sponsored programs. To accelerate the early phase of the mentoring process, program administrators can also distribute the form and explain its purpose at the orientation session for mentees.

Mentee Profile Form

Name:_____**Date:**_____

Career Goals:

Educational Objectives:

Training Plans:

Strategies:

Present Actions:

Available Resources:

Concerns:

*Please provide a summary of your *past:* (1) academic, (2) training, and (3) work background.

Networking

Another useful approach is for mentors to review the available pool of persons and places that mentees should consider meeting with and visiting as sources of information.

The contacts available through the mentor's own work and educational network are often valuable avenues for the mentee to explore in order to gain an insider's view of academic, government, and corporate culture.

Moreover, mentees can usually benefit from the important opportunity to learn the assertive interpersonal lesson that even apparently impenetrable bureaucracy can be accessed by a determined and astute person.

Such a practical lesson can especially serve as a vital insight and motivator to those mentees who, lacking fully developed social skills themselves, become increasingly invested in the denigration of those who succeed in the art of networking. In these cases, mentors can assist mentees in improving their own social competencies by correctly demonstrating that *who* an individual knows can be as important as *what*.

Mentees who do not fully grasp the current reliance in the modern workplace on both effective interpersonal and intergroup interactive skills are definitely candidates for this type of education.

Assessing the Value of Information

In addition to collecting information from the mentee, the mentor will also need to determine the reliability and validity of the reported facts. Moreover, mentors may need to review the individual conclusions arrived at by mentees in utilizing the data to ensure that they have fully understood the implications of the facts that have been selected to guide their decisions.

Mentors must be careful about assuming that because mentees have been successful in finding relevant information that they also can accurately apply the facts to their own special requirements and needs; these activities are not identical. Instead, mentors often need to filter the mentees' data through the lens of their own more comprehensive experience.

Sometimes, mentors need to probe regarding the extent to which the mentees have *realistically interpreted* the facts they are utilizing, especially if the mentees are operating outside of their own particular base of experience and relying primarily on the opinions of others as a substitute for first-hand knowledge.

3. Facilitative Dimension

Key Concept: *Alternatives*

Essential Behaviors:

* Exploring interests/abilities/ ideas/beliefs
* Revealing other views/ attainable objectives
* Discussing own decisions about career/training/education

Introduction

The term *facilitative*, when applied to mentoring, primarily refers to the exploration of a mentee's personal and professional perception of available options. Such a task, however, should be undertaken only *after* the mentor has accumulated enough factual information to ensure that a realistic profile of the mentee has been achieved. In the absence of sufficient knowledge of the mentee, the mentor risks the strong possibility that advice and guidance offered in good faith may have superficial or minimal value, and sometimes, may even contribute to counterproductive decisions.

Sometimes a Difficult Process

By encouraging the examination of alternatives, mentors require that mentees question their ideas, beliefs, and decisions. Although this process is both desirable and necessary, for mentees this specific type of interpersonal engagement is sometimes more difficult than the straightforward review of opinions and attitudes might suggest to the seasoned practitioner.

For example, a genuine exploration of options can create anxiety simply because the attempt itself can be stressful. Mentees are essentially being asked to second-guess their own personal views, so they often need to move outside of their individual comfort zones in order to revisit a variety of fixed positions.

Stress and Education

Such an exploration will prove more emotionally demanding for some mentees than for others; however, mentors should be particularly aware of the possible strain this aspect of the educational journey may create for those mentees with fragile self-confidence.

In addition, in raising issues that involve projecting into the future by referencing the past and present, even the mentor's reasoned and careful introduction of the *what if?* approach can create unease for the mentee.

Value of Discomfort

Although this may not be a problem for most, for some mentees, the response to the exploration of work, education, and career options will create a definite feeling of disturbance. In such instances, mentors can consider prefacing the effort to explore alternatives by briefly reviewing the fact that such endeavors sometimes do trigger additional stress.

Of course, legitimate discomfort is often a necessary ingredient in serious encounters with oneself and others, and anticipated anxiety reactions by a mentee should not automatically be viewed as grounds for terminating the activity.

Learning to Interpret Stress

By honestly engaging in realistic and reasoned exchanges with mentors, mentees can better understand how to interpret their own reactions to stressful events as *alert signals* rather than as the ringing bells of imminent failure.

For mentees, these dialogues can be a vital component of learning how to avoid the immobilizing trap of risk avoidance often caused by an unreflective response to difficult experiences. If not corrected, this type of unthinking, almost programmed reaction can create serious self-doubt for mentees regarding their own capacity to handle future events.

In this regard, constructive and supportive feedback can be a particularly valuable aspect of personal development for mentees who desire to strengthen their own ability at problem solving and decision making so they can negotiate more maturely through the empirical world of unavoidable stress.

Protecting Mentee Decisions

The final arbiter of the mentee's journey is the mentee. Mentors must therefore be on guard to protect the mentee's right of self-determination.

This cautionary note is not meant to suggest that most mentors will somehow knowingly violate mentees' fundamental responsibility for their own destiny. Rather, it is an acknowledgment that the boundaries of responsibility for crafting a mentee's plan of development are sometimes not crystal clear, nor always distinctly marked with warning lights that lines are about to be, or have been, crossed.

4. Confrontive Dimension

Key Concept: *Challenge*

Essential Behaviors:
* Respecting decisions/actions/ career
* Providing insight into unproductive strategies/ behaviors
* Evaluating need/capacity to change

Introduction

The confrontive dimension of mentoring may be the most difficult to sustain as a positive intervention. It is essential for the mentor to understand that the good faith attempt to challenge the mentee is *not* to be equated with the aggressive verbal and nonverbal behaviors associated with the heated and often hostile debate style of traditional win/lose argumentation. In the mentoring model of learning, the mentor "confronts" by guiding and supporting the mentee in the critical act of self-reflection; stress occurs because the mentor deliberately selects an issue to

examine about which there is an apparent
discrepancy.

For example, the mentee may openly state that
career advancement is highly important, yet not
actively participate in the activities that are
considered to be "promotable behaviors," such as
taking the personal initiative to work longer hours
to complete important projects with high visibility
in the organization.

Although the mentee may have a variety of
explanations for not assuming the additional
workload, the mentor can pursue the point that
career success usually mandates that dedication to
achieving work-related goals takes precedence over
other lifestyle commitments.

The central question for the mentee is: Are you
or are you not prepared to pay the price for the
success you covet? There is, of course, no right
answer; there is only the need for the mentee to
clarify individual life and work values.

Often, mentors assist mentees to determine if
some reasonable "job fit" correlation can be
realistically pursued between the often competing
forces of personal/professional interests and the
actual or probable satisfaction with the
responsibilities, daily work, and demands of a
career choice.

Four Important Variables

Mentors must be prepared to explore the
substantial gray area of the real world rather than
settle for the illusory comfort of simple black and
white solutions which may be preferred by
mentees. To be effective in the subtle art of

constructive confrontation, the mentor must therefore demonstrate competence in handling four important variables:

(1) identifying an unproductive mentee idea, behavior, or strategy, which if unchallenged, may create the mistaken impression of mentor agreement and thus the false message of concurrence with a self-defeating approach

(2) engaging in an intellectual dialogue about a serious topic that also usually involves some reasonable degree of mentee ego investment, and thus may very quickly trigger defensive responses

(3) questioning the mentee's experience and judgment by pointing out inconsistencies arising from such complex causes as inadequate facts, misinterpreted information, limited knowledge, or distorted perception

(4) determining that the actual challenge occurs at a point in the interpersonal relationship of probable receptivity, which therefore requires that the mentor be especially alert to the joint problem of coordinating the development of mentee trust with the proper timing of the confrontation

Respect as a Stabilizer

Perhaps the term that best captures the essential ingredient of this complicated mentoring behavior is still the rather old-fashioned idea of *respect*.

Respectful communication provides considerable impact because it often acts as a vital stabilizing influence during the sometimes turbulent path of examining assumptions. Such a route can be particularly difficult if the challenge also involves probing the personal beliefs that have served the purpose of contributing to patterns of avoidance and denial.

The mentor must engage in confrontation about important concerns with patience, sensitivity, and a nonjudgmental attitude that differentiates between acceptance of the mentee and critical scrutiny of the point under review. All of the mentor's verbal and nonverbal interpersonal skills will usually be tested in these sometimes emotionally and psychologically delicate situations.

Referral

The mentor should be prepared to refer the mentee to professionals if the specific problem that emerges involves areas that are clearly outside the boundaries of the mentoring relationship, such as serious issues involving personal, marital, family, or social agendas.

Certainly, the mentor should be reasonably familiar with the range of support services and agencies available in the workplace, academic institution, and community in which the mentor programs operate. Usually, such guidance will be provided by those responsible for new and continuing mentor education initiatives.

Sufficient Time to Respond

Because the benefit of mentoring will sometimes involve a long-term change which is not

43

always easily recognizable during the gradually evolving relationship, the mentor may remain uncertain if the attempt to identify discrepancies was worth the possible interpersonal risk. In some cases, however, anticipating immediate mentee feedback to confirm the usefulness of confrontive interaction may not be a realistic expectation.

The mentor may truly need to allow the passage of time to occur, along with a continuing review of needed changes and ongoing encouragement and support, before the genuine value to the mentee's personal and professional development becomes clear.

Insight and Change

Mentors should remember that even in cases where the mentee responds with admirable self-awareness about problems, and formulates reasonable plans to modify unproductive behaviors or strategies, that insight itself is not a guarantee that change will immediately or automatically be the result.

The agreement to pursue new approaches that results from a successful confrontive experience should be viewed as a significant starting point rather than as a completed race.

Certainly, the more ingrained and complex the particular behavior under review, the higher the probability that productive change will evolve as a gradual series of small victories than as a major leap from negative to positive actions. Mentors should therefore attend to the sometimes more mundane and undramatic details of the change process as much as to the ideals that are often characteristic of the lofty rhetoric of confrontive dialogue.

Mentors should remain acutely aware that the confrontive dimension can involve risk to the relationship, and that the decision to pursue it as an option requires that serious consideration be given to the consequences of raising or not raising a specific issue with the mentee.

From the viewpoint of practical application, the conscientious mentor is faced with the decision of evaluating the confrontation in terms of the negative cost to the mentee and the mentoring relationship itself if a worst case scenario occurs, and the positive benefit to the mentee if the attempt contributes to significant personal development and professional opportunity.

Clearly, deferring or taking no action is sometimes as appropriate as pursuing the path of prudent risk.

5. Mentor Model Dimension

Key Concept: *Motivation*

Essential Behaviors:
* Disclosing life experiences as role model
* Personalizing/enriching relationship
* Taking risks/overcoming difficulties

Introduction

The idea of a mentor model certainly refers to the obvious point that the mentor serves in the important capacity of traditional role model for the mentee. However, a critical difference in a planned mentoring program is that the person who consciously elects to serve as a mentor must make a definite commitment of individual time and energy rather than simply function as a possible (and even unaware) influence from a distance.

Mentors are active participants as they accompany mentees on their journeys of professional development in the workplace. In guiding the mentee, the mentor can offer an especially important component to the mix of elements required for the successful pursuit of goals: the motivation to persevere when faced with difficult conditions and personal insecurity.

Motivation

Certainly, the ability to overcome the problems associated with the lengthy passage required to obtain career and educational objectives is a multifaceted endeavor. The daily anxiety, fatigue, and sometimes slow progress usually require periodic recharging of the emotional, psychological, and intellectual batteries.

Although some individuals appear unusually self-sustaining in handling prolonged stress, most mentees will profit from the infusion of positive energy that can flow—sometimes with the potency of a magically renewing elixir—from an enthusiastic mentor who openly communicates belief in the mentee's capacity to succeed.

A genuine voice of direct encouragement, confidently expressing the belief that goals are realistically obtainable, can often prove to be the critical spark needed to reenergize a mentee into continued action.

Value of Self-Disclosure

When mentees question their own competency and suffer from serious self-doubt, the mentor can also be the vital resource who assists them in renewing their faith in themselves.

The source of inspiration that can often provide the mentees with the powerful incentive to move forward is often readily available within the life and workplace experiences of the mentors, who by example, can demonstrate that they understand what the mentee is feeling and thinking because they have also faced similar obstacles. The value of this self-disclosure is usually not so much in the interesting details of the narrative, nor in the extent to which there is similarity between the mentor's history and the mentee's current situation. Rather, the power to motivate often occurs due to the (sometimes startling for the mentee) revelation that esteemed mentors have also felt the internal chill caused by a loss of self-confidence, but have nonetheless managed to solve difficult problems and reach their goals.

There are individuals, unfortunately, who have become obsessed with their "failures" and are unable to recognize or accept legitimate praise for their achievements. What they have not done, or still need to accomplish, dominates their internal radar screen, while their noteworthy attainments are almost invisible as positive reference points. Some mentees may even need to learn how to properly celebrate their own hard-won success.

The central idea worth internalizing for mentees, of course, is that people who repeatedly strive to achieve become more skilled at mastering the art of survival because they allow themselves to learn—to discover through experience that they can handle a variety of unsettling personal concerns such as ongoing uncertainty and discomfort. Some mentees will need to be gently prodded if they are to comprehend that they must accept rather than hide from challenge. The truism that "Nothing succeeds like success" is no less relevant because it is considered to be conventional wisdom.

Timely self-disclosure can also help those mentees who are secretly agonizing about being somehow "defective" to recognize the myth that they alone are uniquely insecure while others who achieve their goals appear do so happily, with minimum anxiety, and are truly unmistakable towers of perpetual public and private strength.

Especially for mentees with distorted viewpoints, the art of useful self-disclosure will depend on the ability of the mentor to select and share relevant stories that will resonant with productive meaning within each distinct individual.

Issues of Disclosure

Although this particular type of shared relationship—which offers more genuine one-to-one involvement—usually provides the mentee with a significant opportunity for positive growth, there is also a higher potential for interpersonal friction. In fact, such a situation can occur *because* mentors gradually reveal themselves to be more human—more vulnerable—than mentees are sometimes prepared to accept, especially if the mentor represents an idealized figure of success.

Mentors who enter the world of self-disclosure may discover that some mentees are actually more comfortable viewing them through the lens of unrealistic rather than realistic expectations. For some mentees, the desire to believe that the mentor is in total control of events and can triumph no matter how threatening the scenario is almost like the fantasies that temporarily soothe a child into a false sense of security. As protector, the mentor could then be interpreted as the mentee's emotional/psychological equivalent of a "security blanket," even though such a viewpoint would not be particularly attractive to a professional whose own sense of identity and worth derive from a quite different perception.

Although most mentees will be more mature and less dependent than the extreme case posed by the insecure and naive person alluded to above, mentors should be aware that even reasonably confident mentees may react with conflicting emotions to the discovery that mentors have "clay feet." On the positive side, those mentees who have suffered from the destructive error of believing that "perfect" is actually an obtainable standard may benefit from awakening to a more accurate picture of the world, and thereby gain a more productive image of others and of themselves.

Obtaining a healthy insight into the actual lives of successful human beings—who are, of course, less than perfect—can often be a salutary learning experience for mentees who have previously believed in powerfully self-limiting nonsense, and may therefore have been debilitated or diminished as a result of bad or careless advice, flawed perceptions, and unfounded beliefs.

On the problematic side, however, the task of constructively differentiating real from idealized people may require a substantial commitment by the mentor. Mentees may undergo a substantial struggle in coming to terms with immature ideas or inadequate beliefs. For example, in traveling this difficult pathway, some mentees may even be both attracted to as well as repelled by the variety of conflicts (intrapersonal as well as interpersonal) such issues can trigger. In certain cases, the mentor may even need to consider referring a mentee with complicated emotional issues to a specialized professional.

However, because the development of clear-headed insight is of great potential value to the mentee, mentors should not be reluctant to engage mentees in an examination of those cherished but dysfunctional beliefs that are based on misperceptions about the world.

Dealing with Risk

The idea of "taking a risk" is a more complicated point than it sometimes appears to be in our competitive environment. For some mentees, it is not about rather straightforward decisions and subsequent actions. Instead, to actually engage in what could quite reasonably be viewed by many as a prudent risk involves the difficult hurdle of overcoming subjective as well as objective obstacles. In fact, to the mentor, the mentee's reluctance to pursue a clearly defined action may appear to be a puzzling overreaction.

However, such inability to act may often be explained by what the current "risk" represents to the mentee; those with a painful history of lack of demonstrated success can gradually become "risk avoidant." So the risk of racking up another personal or professional "failure"—even if not viewed as a major issue from the perspective of the mentor—can often grow out of proportion in magnitude as an ego threat to the mentee who is hesitant to pursue more failure. Even a "lightweight" failure can therefore assume significant weight to a mentee already burdened with a previous load of negative experience.

Mentors should be especially patient in helping mentees to develop realistic assessments of risk. Often, this type of learning begins with a review of the basics, including an initial clarification of the meaning of "risk" as personally defined by the mentee. The mentor's own stories about learning how to constructively deal with the risk to the ego of mistakes and missteps can be highly significant as a source of pragmatic motivational advice.

Personalize the Relationship

Personalizing the relationship in mentoring should be understood as the willingness of mentors to reveal aspects of their own private struggles to obtain educational and career goals. These stories, which clearly require a more intimate type of self-disclosure, however, are carefully selective and primarily directed at the objective of allowing mentees to recognize that success is achieved by normal human beings who must deal with their own personal vulnerabilities, not superhuman figures who float ever confident above the fray.

In forging a relationship in which the interpersonal bonds are definite and positive, the mentor is not trying to duplicate the intimate type of contact that is characteristic of more reciprocal types of involvement, such as that of romantic, close friendship, or family. Instead, the assumption underlying the mentoring model of learning is that the mentor is primarily responsible for investing time and energy in promoting the mentee's educational and career growth, rather than the reverse. The "needs" of the mentor are considered to be a secondary, and in some cases, inappropriate focus of their mutual professional interaction.

It is the mentee who is rightfully the proper beneficiary of the mentoring experience—whose individual needs are of paramount importance rather than those of the mentor. In addressing the mentee's specific developmental concerns, mentors therefore attempt to be of direct help by disclosing important details of their own relevant private histories. Such assistance is often valuable to the mentee in two related and important ways, because it allows the mentee:

(1) to gain insight into the often hidden "behind the scenes" strategies individuals must develop in managing real-world conditions

(2) to formulate coping skills appropriate for their own unique personalities and individual lifestyle, career, and workplace situations

Certainly, with careful attention to the motivational value of the personal story that is shared, the mentor model dimension can be a profoundly influential experience for the mentee, often with subtle and long-lasting inspirational significance.

6. Employee Vision Dimension

Key Concept: *Initiative*

Essential Behaviors:
* Thinking critically about career future
* Realizing personal/professional potential
* Initiating change/negotiating transitions

Introduction

Employee vision is usually associated with the final phase of mentor-mentee involvement. However, from the perspective of career and educational planning, important concerns can certainly be raised about the future in the initial and middle as well as in the later stages of mentoring.

Although some of the decisions and actions that result from early interactions will clearly have short-term and limited agendas, some plans will also involve the gradual building of the solid foundation on which longer-term objectives depend for completion. Mentors should therefore consider issues connected to the employee vision dimension as a relevant topic for critical reflection during any phase of the mentoring relationship.

Mentee Potential

The subject of mentee potential raises two immediate questions regarding the pursuit of career and educational goals:

(1) Do the plans reveal a reasonable correlation between the mentee's intellectual, psychological, and emotional profile and the stated objectives?
(2) Has the mentee developed realistic strategies and identified reliable resources to support their attainment?

In situations where the mentee's aptitude and maturity are consistent with the targeted objectives and indicate a "good fit," the mentor should find that responding in the affirmative to the mentee's plans will often be a rather clear-cut decision.

An obvious concern, of course, even in a more apparently straightforward instance, is that mentors still accurately assess the extent to which mentees are truly pursuing goals that will allow them to maximize their specific talents—that their ability and ambition are matched.

Mentor Reservations

However, if the mentor is not completely confident in the mentee's capacity to complete the envisioned agenda, then the obligation to offer honest feedback can suddenly be transformed into a significant source of possible friction. An important guideline, therefore, is to remember that even after forming a skeptical assessment of the mentee's plans, mentors are not automatically required to immediately transmit their reactions. In these cases, mentors will often need to tread very carefully with regard to openly questioning mentees' abilities to accomplish their stated career and educational objectives.

Generally, this type of volatile issue would have surfaced (and hopefully been resolved) well before the later phases of mentoring, although some mentees may insist on periodically revisiting prior agendas until the very last stages of the relationship. Also, in the early stages of mentoring, most mentors would have already found that the cautious approach was the practical brake which prevented them from commenting too quickly—and therefore possibly unwisely—regarding their doubts about their mentees' plans.

Mentors need to be fully attuned to the mistakes awaiting those who proffer instant advice to mentees with whom they are just becoming acquainted, and to fully recognize those interpersonal situations in which they have not yet accumulated enough substantive information.

But as the mentoring relationship evolves, and the mentor develops a reasonably well-defined profile of the mentee, then the mentor may actually be faced with the problem of whether or not to agree with the mentee's openly expressed hopes for the future.

If the past record, as well as the the present evidence, indicate that mentees have formed highly unrealistic goals which will be extremely difficult to accomplish, then the mentor must make a judgment about what action to take at that point in the relationship. The mentor must determine the most helpful strategy: Would it be beneficial or not to confront the mentee?

Communicating Concern

The dilemma, of course, for the mentor involves the difficult task of remaining a positive advocate for the mentee while also fulfilling the mandate of offering the best possible advice based on careful observations, sufficient information, and honest conclusions.

One pragmatic solution to the problem is to allow mentees the opportunity to *test* their own plans in the world so that they can obtain the necessary personal and professional reference points that are often a prerequisite for meaningful self-realization.

This is an especially valuable learning pathway, especially if the mistakes are not particularly costly, the mentees will recover from the experience with their egos sufficiently intact, and the probability is high that they will regain their balance and continue on their journey, perhaps with modified maps.

Consequences of Avoidance

Sometimes, in difficult situations, especially with mentees struggling with emotional issues, it may be very hard for the mentor to confront the mentee when the occasion really requires it, but the mentor risks becoming a participant in collusion by avoiding confrontation.

Certainly, some mentees may apply their own pressure to avoid dealing directly with the unpleasant side of reality, and even resist directly considering what mentors truly believe to be accurate and well-reasoned viewpoints.

However, if the mentor chooses to confirm a mentee's unrealistic and unsupportable plans by temporarily engaging in the wishful hope that somehow everything will magically work out in the end, then the mentor may actually contribute in a negative manner by inadvertently enabling mentees to continue their unproductive dependence on fantasy.

If the opportune moment never arrives, and the scenario degenerates into endless delays, mentor patience and empathy may turn into avoidance. In some cases, this inaction allows preventable damage to occur, seriously undermining what began as a good faith act of healthy nurturing.

Advocacy Viewpoint

Mentors clearly want to support positive initiatives and to encourage rather than discourage mentees from pursuing their chosen paths, even if there is concern about the probability of successful results.

This is why—from the advocacy viewpoint which is the rationale behind the mentoring relationship—the act of "brutally" deflating the mentee's ego over the issue of ability versus goals under the guise of "for the mentee's own benefit" serves no legitimate or constructive purpose.

Such an aggressive confrontive action would normally be contrary to the mentor's obligation to behave in a manner consistent with the role of advocate, and therefore viewed as counter-productive to the mentee's welfare. The assumption of mentoring is that the hard realities of the world-at-large will provide ample opportunities for mentees to experience assaults on their self-confidence. Generally, mentors therefore support the initiatives of mentees, even though they also offer honest opinions about the wisdom of their decisions.

With respect to reviewing the art of interpersonal candor, mentors can refer for additional guidance to the material covered in the section on the confrontive dimension. This approach is particularly applicable to handling sensitive implications regarding career and educational plans.

Initiating and Managing Change

For some mentees, the process of implementing their plans will be a difficult challenge. A clear issue for mentors will be assisting mentees who appear in cognitive control of the information and reasonably comfortable with the decisions, but who repeatedly do not follow-through on their own expressed intentions. If mentees understand what is required, why are they unable to take the actions required by their own education, workplace training, or career development plans?

From the standpoint of the human personality, the answer may be rather complex, but with respect to the mentoring relationship, the mentor

59

can attempt reasonable interventions, as well as consider referring the mentee to a specialist if the occasion requires it.

Sometimes, the problem is more obvious, and can be explained by a mentee's initial stress reaction as the pressure from the demands of new and multiple work and educational commitments rapidly builds, increases, and continues unabated.

As mentees regain their balance and confidence, however, their ability to learn and utilize effective coping strategies—especially with mentor advice and support during the period of change—usually provides the stability necessary for them to persevere and succeed. Also, most mentees can usually transfer such learning and independently pursue positive initiatives and productively manage their transitions through a variety of future events.

But for those mentees who are still struggling to achieve the balance required to formulate mature decisions and to pursue professional achievement, mentors may need to provide more direct support in the present as well as to assist more proactively with planning for the future.

Mentor Satisfaction with Results

With regard to documentable results, mentors should note that when mentees' major outcomes are finally realized, they may no longer be directly involved in formal mentoring relationships. Such a situation usually will be the case in programs of relatively limited duration, such as those in which the participants are paired for less than a year.

In certain instances, mentors should be prepared to wait patiently for the personal satisfaction that they derive from sharing in the ultimate success of their mentees. Mentors sometimes become so immersed in events along the pathway toward the mentees' destination that they sometimes miss the gratification that should be derived from positive feedback about the smaller daily achievements of less dramatic steps on the route.

Maintaining Records of Mentoring Sessions

Maintaining Records of Mentoring Sessions

Purpose of Notes

After each meeting with a mentee, the mentor should record the essential issues and actions that have been covered at that specific session, as well as create a log of agendas that have been agreed on for later review. In addition, the mentor may include notes for points that were not raised (for many reasons) but that might be suitable topics for the future.

The following form for recording mentoring sessions can be used as a model.

Mentoring Session Record

Mentor_____**Date**_____

Mentee_____**Session**_____

Topics Covered at Present Session

Present Issues:

Current Actions:

Future Agendas:

Other Subjects:

Topics for Later Reference

◻✳

Mentee Learning Activities

Mentee Learning Activities

Introduction

There are usually numerous learning activities available for mentees to pursue. Abundant opportunities, for example, currently exist within the modern workplace, in formal institutions of education, and in the informal network of community-based programs.

In addition, the proliferation of entrepreneurial and professional organizations that conduct specialized training seminars, the variety of self-paced computer and video programs, and the growing number of new interactive sources for instruction and information offered on the Internet, have created a rapidly expanding world of possibilities for acquiring additional critical skills, as well as for developing the fine-tuned proficiencies required to compete in both a technologically advanced and a behaviorally complex environment.

Mentees, of course, will vary in sophistication regarding their perception of viable learning opportunities. Also, the specific context of each mentee could be considerably different, ranging from more experienced staff who have been selected for highly competitive leadership development programs, to those at entry-level positions who are still learning the essentials of their job.

Mentors should engage mentees in serious dialogues to determine the most productive pathways for obtaining learning relevant to the workplace. All possible avenues of education should be examined to ensure that the mentee's potential for learning is maximized.

The following list contains suggested activities that mentors might also participate in with their mentees:

(1) college courses
(2) computer software programs
(3) television/distance education
(4) relevant books/journals
(5) structured on-the-job training
(6) job sponsored seminars/workshops
(7) job rotational assignments
(8) internships
(9) workplace meetings
(10) sales (and other types of) presentations
(11) professional societies
(12) special projects
(13) interviews of personnel/training specialists
(14) networking
(15) researching career/educational options
(16) participating in work-related organizations

A Practitioner's Reference: Utilizing the *Principles of Adult Mentoring Inventory*

A Practitioner's Reference:
Utilizing the *Principles of Adult Mentoring Inventory*

Purpose of Practitioner's Reference

The *Principles of Adult Mentoring Inventory* (*PAMI*) was developed to provide professional staff with a self-assessment instrument for evaluating their own effectiveness as mentors of adult learners. The inventory is based on the concept that the complete mentor role consists of six distinct but related dimensions of behavioral competencies. The *PAMI* is available for mentors to take, self-score, and interpret in booklet form.

The purpose of a separate Practitioner's Reference to Utilizing the *Principles of Adult Mentoring Inventory* is to offer a guide which is logically organized to provide practical access to the 55 statements of the inventory. The statements included in the *PAMI* directly reflect core mentor behaviors, and collectively represent a profile of the interpersonal competencies a mentor would demonstrate in fulfilling the complete mentor role.

The original inventory presented the information in random order, but the Practitioner's Reference groups each of the 55 statements under one of the six separate mentoring dimensions.

This format offers mentors more practical access to the material, which can now be utilized as a compendium of highly significant mentoring behaviors. Mentors can also review the *PAMI* with special attention to those areas of specific mentoring competency that require improvement.

While it is certainly possible to use the Practitioner's Reference as a compressed education in the art of mentoring without taking the inventory, mentors are definitely encouraged to first use the *PAMI* as a self-assessment instrument, and afterwards to rely on the approach offered by the reference as a source for understanding and applying the principles in their actual face-to-face interaction with mentees.

Organization of Material

The following section groups each of the 55 separate inventory statements under one of the six distinct dimensions of corresponding mentor behavior.

All 55 inventory statements are listed along with their actual numbers.

However, in order to increase its convenience as a workable reference for the practitioner, the information in the original *PAMI* has been reformatted and sometimes slightly modified.

The content, of course, directly reflects the intent of the original statements. Italics have also been added to highlight key aspects of each mentor behavior.

In addition, summaries of the critical points relevant to the six mentoring dimensions and associated inventory statements have been included in the Practitioner's Reference to Utilizing the *PAMI*.

1. Relationship Dimension

1. I encourage employees to express their *honest feelings* (positive or negative) about their work-related experiences, including such dimensions as
    *training
    *educational opportunities
    *social relationships.

5. I attempt to be *verbally supportive*
    *when employees are emotionally upset.

7. I make a good deal of *eye contact* with employees
    *during our meetings.

12. I explain to employees that I really want to know what they as individuals *honestly think*, so that I can offer advice specific to them about issues such as
    *balancing job requirements/career development commitments with responsibilities outside of the workplace.

13. I arrange my meetings with employees at times when I will probably *not be interrupted* by
    *telephone calls
    *anticipated personal contacts by other staff.

23. I verbally communicate my concerns to employees when their *negative attitudes and emotions* are expressed to me through such nonverbal behaviors as
     *eye contact
     *facial expression
     *voice tone.

42. I *listen to criticism* from employees about work-related policies, regulations, requirements, and even colleagues
     *without immediately attempting to offer justifications.

44. I inform employees that in our meetings they can discuss *"negative" emotions* which are directly related to the workplace, such as
     *anxiety
     *self-doubt
     *fear
     *anger.

47. I discuss the *positive and negative feelings* employees have about their
     *own abilities to succeed in their careers.

53. I try to *clarify the problems* employees are explaining to me
     *by verbally expressing my understanding of their feelings
     *then asking if my views are accurate.

Summary of Relationship Statements

(1) *honest feelings—regarding work

(5) *verbally supportive

(7) *eye contact

(12) *honestly think—career vs. personal life

(13) *not be interrupted—calls/staff

(23) *negative attitudes/emotions—nonverbal

(42) *listen to criticism

(44) *negative emotions—about workplace

(47) *positive/negative feelings—about abilities

(53) *clarify problems—verbal check

2. Informative Dimension

3. I ask employees for *detailed information* about
*their progress in learning all aspects of their
job.

4. I *refer employees* to other staff members and
departments to obtain information relevant to
pursuing their individual goals for
*education
*training
*career development.

6. I suggest to employees that we establish a
regular
*schedule of meeting times.

9. I ask employees to identify *career choices* as well
as to explain their own *strategies* for continuing
their work-related training and learning
*to support the achievement of these career
goals.

10. I encourage employees to provide a good deal of
background information about the pursuit of their
career goals, such as
*preparation
*success
*problems.

11. I inquire in some depth about employees'
strategies for utilizing *workplace resources* to

increase their on-the-job learning, and when
appropriate
    *offer practical suggestions
    *refer them for assistance to improve their job
     performance.

19. I offer recommendations to employees about
their *current and future training and educational*
needs (from basic to advanced skills and learning)
based on specific information provided by them
regarding their own history of previous
    *training
    *experience
    *academic/technical preparation.

24. I discuss employees' general reasons for
planning to obtain additional work-related
educational *credentials or training* and then focus
on helping them identify concrete
    *degrees
    *curricula
    *courses
    *workshops.

40. I assist employees in using facts to carefully
map out *realistic step-by-step strategies* to achieve
their
    *career
    *training
    *educational goals.

52. I discuss my *role as a mentor* with employees
so that their individual expectations of me are
    *appropriate
    *realistic.

Summary of Informative Statements

(3) *detailed information—
     progress learning job

(4) *refer employees—other
     staff/departments

(6) *regular—meeting schedule

(9) *career choices—training/
     learning strategies

(10) *background—career goals

(11) *workplace resources—on-
     the-job training

(19) *training/education—
     current/future

(24) *credentials/training—
     concrete sources

(40) *realistic step-by-step
     strategies—map out

(52) *role as mentor—expectations

3. Facilitative Dimension

15. I encourage employees to consider formal educational opportunities to develop their career interests as well as *nontraditional and distance education* courses, such as those offered through
  *television
  *correspondence
  *Internet.

22. I attempt to guide employees who are currently exploring their own commitment to career and work-related educational interests by posing *alternative views*, such as considering other
  *career
  *training
  *education options.

25. I provide a reasonable amount of *factual guidance* in our discussions so that employees will explore
  *realistic options
  *attainable career objectives.

34. I encourage employees to use me as a *sounding board* to explore their work-related
  *hopes
  *ideas
  *feelings
  *plans.

39. I explore with employees who express a *lack of confidence* in themselves the ways in which their own life experiences might be a valuable resource to help them
    *devise strategies to succeed within the workplace environment.

49. I ask probing questions that require *more than a "yes" or "no" answer* so that employees will explain in some detail their views regarding their career
    *plans
    *progress.

Summary of Facilitative Statements

(15) *nontraditional/distance—consider

(22) *alternative views—career/education

(25) *factual guidance—examine options

(34) *sounding board—explore workplace

(39) *lack of confidence—experience as resource

(49) *more than yes/no answer—career goals and progress

4. Confrontive Dimension

8. I suggest to employees who indicate concerns about serious *emotional or psychological problems* that they
> *meet with a counselor responsible for assisting employees
> *consult with a professional outside the workplace.

16. I point out *inconsistencies* (rationalizations) in employees' explanations of why their job performance and career goals were not achieved if I believe my comments will help them to
> *develop better coping strategies to deal with their problems.

18. I explain to employees why they should share (even suggesting someone other than myself) significant *work-related problems* they are presently confronted with
> *even if they prefer not to directly deal with these issues.

21. I tell employees when I think their ideas about career or educational concerns are very clearly based on *incomplete or inaccurate* information regarding such topics as
> *promotional opportunity
> *entry into a different job
> *future training
> *degree requirements.

27. I guide employees through a *review of personal experiences and specific facts* they are using to base their ideas and beliefs on, especially with regard to important topics such as their
    *career options
    *individual views about the purpose of
      education.

31. I point out, using personal examples as well as anecdotes about other employees, that career achievement is primarily based on *personal commitment and planning* rather than just "luck," especially to those employees having problems completing all of their job projects, training, or educational assignments, but who still appear
    *unrealistic about the amount of discipline
      and energy needed to cope with the pressures
      of contemporary career advancement.

33. I confront employees with the reality of continued or probable negative consequences in a *direct but supportive* manner when they
    *repeatedly do not follow-through on their
      stated intentions to deal with serious job and
      career-related problems.

37. I offer employees constructive criticism if I believe their *avoidance of problems and decisions* is clearly limiting their
    *work performance
    *career potential.

43. I offer comments to employees about what appears to be their own *inappropriate or ineffective*

behavior at work (based on their own explanations and descriptions) if I have a reasonable expectation that they
  *are prepared to work on positive change
  *will most likely experience some success as a result.

46. I question employees' decisions and actions regarding *past and current* work-related issues and problems when they do not appear to have
  *formulated or implemented appropriate solutions.

48. I offer as few *carefully chosen criticisms* as possible when I try to get employees to understand the often difficult to accept connection between their
  *own self-limiting (defeating) behaviors and their inability to solve a particular work-related problem.

51. I base the *timing* (often related to the stage of our relationship) of my "confrontive" questions and comments on my knowledge of the employee's individual readiness to
  *benefit from discussions about clearly sensitive work-related issues.

Summary of Confrontive Statements

- (8) *psychological/emotional problems—refer to appropriate help
- (16) *inconsistencies—job/career goals
- (18) *work problems—share with others
- (21) *incomplete/inaccurate information—career/education
- (27) *review experiences/facts—ideas/beliefs
- (31) *commitment/planning—not luck
- (33) *direct but supportive—if no follow-up
- (37) *avoidance of problems/decisions—limitations of

(43) *inappropriate/ineffective
behavior—work
(46) *past/current work
problems—solutions
(48) *careful criticisms—about
behaviors
(51) *timing—knowledge of
individual readiness

5. Mentor Model Dimension

2. I discuss with employees who are discouraged due to lack of promotion or other difficulties the importance of developing a realistic view of work-related advancement that can include both *success and disappointment*, mentioning, for example

    *other employees who have been frustrated but still continued to explore opportunities to learn and enhance their marketable knowledge, skills, and behaviors at work.

28. I discuss *my own work-related experience* as a way of helping employees think about and carefully examine

    *their specific career options.

29. I share with employees *personal examples of difficulties I have overcome* in my own individual and professional growth if

    *these experiences might provide insights for them.

32. I express *my personal confidence* in the ability of employees to succeed if they

    persevere in the pursuit of their career goals.

36. I use *my own experience* (personal as well as references to other employees I have advised) to explain how opportunities that employees believe will not be career-relevant could in fact be valuable work-related learning experiences for them, mentioning topics such as
     *training workshops
     *educational programs
     *job rotations.

41. I share *my own views and feelings* when they are relevant to the
       *work-related situations and issues I am
        discussing with employees.

Summary of Mentor Model Statements

- (2) *success/disappointment—realistic views
- (28) *own work experience—examine options
- (29) *difficulties overcome—share insights
- (32) *personal confidence—achieve career goals
- (36) *my own experience—view of opportunities
- (41) *own views/feelings—relevance to their situation/issues

6. Employee Vision Dimension

14. I point out to employees the importance of obtaining accurate and detailed information about their *career options*, especially those who still have insufficient factual information about issues such as

   *additional or changing work-related training and educational requirements
   *preparing for the personal psychological and emotional transition between job fields.

17. I try to stimulate employees to do more rigorous critical thinking about the long-range implications their career choices may pose for *increasing the complexity of their lives* (such as requiring more time and energy commitments for training and education), in order to help them
   *plan
   *prepare
   *adapt to "predictable" lifestyle changes.

20. I follow up on employees' stated goals to develop better personal decision-making strategies relevant to *career and educational planning*, such as obtaining current information and researching multiple sources, by asking questions and offering comments about their
   *actual progress at later meetings.

26. I ask employees to review their plans for *managing the current or anticipated changes* in their personal lives, such as the impact of increased pressures on their own family and social relationships, while they pursue
    *their specific job and career-related
      educational goals.

30. I engage employees in discussions which require them to reflect on the *new competencies* they will need to
    *achieve their future goals.

35. I engage employees in discussions aimed at motivating them to develop a *positive view of their ability* to function now and in the future
    *as independent, competent adult learners in
      the workplace environment.

38. I encourage employees to make *well-informed and critically reflective* personal choices as they plan their
    *career experience
    *training
    *educational goals.

45. I express *confidence in employees' abilities* to achieve their career-related educational and training goals, especially when they are having personal difficulties in fulfilling their educational responsibilities due to pressures from
    *work
    *family
    *social relationships.

50. I explore with employees the extent of their own *commitment* to achieving career goals, reviewing (if necessary) issues regarding their own individual willingness to spend time and energy as adult learners in pursuing such activities as
   *job-related training
   *continuing education.

54. I ask employees to reflect on and explore the *resources* available to help them manage the change and stress in their lives more effectively while they pursue their career and educational goals, such as
      *government-sponsored training and assistance
      *college courses and programs
      *community-based organizations and workshops
      *family and social relationships.

55. I emphasize to employees, especially those who appear *uncertain* about what to expect from our meetings, that one of my important objectives as a mentor is to be of assistance to them in their personal progress toward
      *training
      *education
      *career goals.

Summary of Employee Vision Statements

(14) *career options—accurate information

(17) *increased complexity of life—career choices

(20) *career/education plans—goals/strategies

(26) *managing changes—personal/social impact

(30) *new competencies—future goals

(35) *positive view of ability—motivate/develop

(38) *informed/reflective choices—individual plans

(45) *confidence in ability—deal with difficulty

(50) *commitment to career—energy/time

(54) *resources—manage change/ stress
(55) *uncertain expectation— progress/goals

A Concise View of the Six Mentoring Dimensions

A Concise View of the Six Mentoring Dimensions

Introduction
    The following material should provide the practitioner with a compressed yet comprehensive understanding of the overall approach to mentoring referred to as the *complete* mentor role. Italics are used to identify essential points.

Relationship Dimension

* Practice *empathetic* listening (verbal and nonverbal behaviors that signal sincere interest).

* Ask *open-ended* questions related to expressed immediate concerns about actual situations.

* Provide *descriptive* feedback based on observations rather than inferences of motives.

* Use *perception* checks to ensure comprehension of feelings.

* Offer *nonjudgmental*, sensitive responses to assist in clarification of emotional states and reactions.

Informative Dimension

* Ask questions aimed at assuring factual understanding of *present* job and career situation.

* Review relevant *background* to develop adequate work-related personal profile.

* Ask *probing* questions which require concrete answers.

* Offer *directive-type* comments about present problems and solutions that should be considered.

* Make *restatements* to ensure factual accuracy and clarity of interpretive understanding.

* Rely on *facts* as an integral component of decision making.

Facilitative Dimension

* Pose *hypothetical questions* to expand individual views.

* Uncover underlying experiential and informational basis for *assumptions*.

* Present *multiple viewpoints* to generate more in-depth analysis of decisions and options.

* Examine the seriousness of *commitment* to goals.

* Analyze *reasons* for current pursuits.

* Review specific work-related *preferences* and career interests.

Confrontive Dimension

* Use careful *probing* to assess psychological readiness to benefit from different points of view.

* Make open *acknowledgement* of concerns about possible negative consequences of constructive criticism on relationship.

* Employ a confrontive verbal stance aimed at promoting self-assessment of *discrepancies* between career goals and commitment, strategies, and actions to achieve objectives.

* Select most likely *behaviors* and strategies for meaningful change.

* Use the *least* amount of carefully stated constructive criticism necessary for impact.

* Offer comments (before and after confrontive remarks) to reinforce belief in positive *potential* for growth beyond current situation.

Mentor Model Dimension

* Offer personal *thoughts* and genuine *feelings* to emphasize value of work-related learning from unsuccessful or difficult experiences (as trial, error, and self-correction and not as growth-limiting failures).

* Select *related* examples from own life (and experiences as mentor of other employees) based on probable motivational value.

* Provide a direct, positive belief in employees through *realistic* assessment of their ability to commit to and achieve attainable goals.

* Express a *confident* view of appropriate "risk-taking" as necessary to pursue opportunities for personal, training, educational, and career development.

* Make statements that clearly encourage personal *actions* to fulfill expressed objectives.

Employee Vision Dimension

* Make statements that require reflection on *present and future* career, training, and educational attainments.

* Ask questions aimed at clarifying perceptions (positive and negative) about personal ability to manage *change*.

* Review individual *choices* based on a reasonable assessment of options and resources.

* Make comments directed at analysis of problem-solving and decision-making *strategies*.

* Express *confidence* in carefully thought out decisions.

* Offer remarks that show respect for employees' *capacity* to determine their own future.

* Encourage employees to develop talents and pursue *dreams*.

Subject Index

About the Author

Norman H. Cohen is a professor at the Community College of Philadelphia. He received his bachelor's degree in English from Washington College and master's degree in English from Temple University. Dr. Cohen also earned a Doctorate in Adult Education and Psychology from Temple University, Department of Curriculum, Instruction, & Technology. He has conducted research, presented many papers and seminars at major conferences, published numerous articles, and authored two books, ***Mentoring Adult Learners: A Guide for Educators and Trainers*** (Krieger Publishing Company, 1995) and ***Mentoring: New Strategies and Challenges*** (with Dr. Michael Galbraith, Jossey-Bass Publishers, 1995).

Dr. Cohen, a principal in **The Center for Professional Mentoring**, has worked extensively as a consultant with a wide range of business, government, educational, military, religious, community, and health care organizations. Many doctoral dissertations have been completed which utilized Dr. Cohen's books on mentoring theory and practice, with particular use of the ***Principles of Adult Mentoring Inventory***. A variety of institutions have incorporated the inventory and books into their orientation and training programs for mentors, mentees, and program coordinators.

His most recent publications are ***The Principles of Adult Mentoring Inventory***, 1998 (self-assessment instrument, interpretation, and implications for mentor-employee relationship), ***The Mentor Critique Form***, 1998 (instrument and guidance for use in group training workshops), ***The Leader's Guide to the Principles of Adult Mentoring Inventory and the Mentor Critique Form***, 1998, ***The Manager's Pocket Guide to Mentoring***, 1999, ***The Mentees Guide to Mentoring***, 1999, and ***Becoming a Mentor: A Video Based Workshop***, 2000 (includes leader's guide and participant workbook), all of which are available from HRD Press.